BURN THE FAIRY TALES 2

ADELINE WHITMORE

burn the fairy tales 2

(c) 2019 Adeline Whitmore
all rights reserved

adeline whitmore

dedication

i want to dedicate this book
of poetry to my personal hero,
malala yousafzai. your example
of heroism and tenacity have
been the shining star guiding
me forward for many years.

burn the fairy tales 2

adeline whitmore

TRIGGER WARNINGS

my dear reader, some of the topics i talk about in the poems in this book may be triggering to you if you are sensitive to the topics of rape culture, sexual assault, the me too movement, patriarcical society, and several other related topics. if you might be triggered by these topics, proceed with care. ♡

burn the fairy tales 2

adeline whitmore

TABLE OF CONTENTS

<u>chapter one</u>
cinderella after midnight

<u>chapter two</u>
taking the crown

<u>chapter three</u>
white knight, dark soul

<u>chapter four</u>
her own queen

burn the fairy tales 2

CHAPTER ONE

adeline whitmore

CINDERELLA AFTER MIDNIGHT

burn the fairy tales 2

<u>cinderella after midnight</u>

he only loved her
for the facade of perfection
provided by magic

all he wanted
was to use her

adeline whitmore

<u>always</u>

you have always been beautiful
before anyone
told you
you were

burn the fairy tales 2

they would do anything
before
they acknowledge
that women's complaints
about living
in modern society
are valid

adeline whitmore

you will never
take away my voice
no matter how hard
you try

burn the fairy tales 2

they say
we don't have the money
for universal health care

but they have
no hesitation
about spending money
on bombs and missiles

adeline whitmore

being poor
in america
is a death sentence

burn the fairy tales 2

rise up
against the forces
of evil
that control our world

we may not succeed
but history
will never forgive us
if we do not
try

do not
for a second
lose your faith
in the process of life

life
will lead you
exactly
where you need
to go

burn the fairy tales 2

do not allow society
to dictate to you
what about your body
you are allowed
to think is beautiful

you are beautiful-
every scar
every wrinkle
every bit of cellulite.

slurs

society
will never get tired
of finding
new labels
to hurt women
for anything and everything
they do

don't waste your time

don't waste your time
on men
who only want to use you
and give nothing back

the sun
will rise
in the morning

and you
will rise
with it

burn the fairy tales 2

a selfish lover
is acting
out of beliefs
that go much deeper

if he only cares
about his orgasm
and doesn't care
about yours

he views you
as a piece of meat
for his use
and not
a human being

<u>love yourself</u>

the world
will try to convince you
that you do not deserve
to love yourself

but you
must never
let them convince you
that their bullshit
is the truth

burn the fairy tales 2

her skimpy outfit
didn't assault her

her drinking
didn't assault her

a man
assaulted her;
and yet
society
wants to blame
her.

aziz ansari

these fake feminist males
co-opt the movement
for their own gain

but then
as soon as they are caught
not practicing
what they preach
they turn on us

showing us
who they really were
all along

CHAPTER TWO

adeline whitmore

TAKING THE CROWN

burn the fairy tales 2

the only one you need
to defend you
is your own
damn self

adeline whitmore

let us teach
our daughters
from a young age
that they can be
anything they want
to be

burn the fairy tales 2

you do not exist
for the pleasure of men
to be used
as some romantic object
a golden shackle

life is short
be reckless
take care of yourself
and go after
what you want

what are you waiting for?

burn the fairy tales 2

if the person
you're thinking about
hasn't made
the same effort
you make

they just
aren't
as equally invested
as you are

adeline whitmore

do not allow
the weight of your mistakes
to hold you down

burn the fairy tales 2

you deserve
to be treated
with all the softness
and gentleness
you desire

adeline whitmore

put a solar panel
on every roof
of every building
in our biggest cities

it's time
to take climate change
fucking seriously

burn the fairy tales 2

you make me feel safe
even when the world
seems like it may collapse
at any moment

adeline whitmore

you know me
better
than i know myself

you know the waves
of my soul
and you surf them
so effortlessly

burn the fairy tales 2

love
can cast
a lamp
into the most cavernous
darkness

there
is no greater truth
than the simple commandment
that we
must
love
each other

burn the fairy tales 2

the worst thing
you could be
in such a vastly fucked up
world
is
indifferent

all our stories
all our art
all the beauty
we pointed out
in the world

it all adds up
to the simple need
to be understood
and to understand
ourselves

burn the fairy tales 2

never allow
anyone
to tell you
that you
are not enough

a woman
backed into a corner
by the struggles
of life

is like a lioness
in a bamboo cage

if only
she knew
her true
power

burn the fairy tales 2

simple reassurance
is never
too much to ask for

do not waste your time
on men
who will not give you
this simple love

all of humankind
under one roof
one people
unchained to ideology
one glorious sphere
traveling through the cosmos

this is my dream.

<u>do not be silent</u>

if your heart
still beats

you cannot
be silent
about things
that matter.

do not be silent pt. ii

silence
is the enemy
of progress.

<u>controversy</u>

i don't care
if what i say
is controversial

i must say
what i think
and believe

there is no
two ways
about it.

all women, together

feminism
that is not
intersectional
is not truly
feminism
at all.

history

history
will finally
begin to recognize
the contributions
of women

because we
will be the ones
to force history
to remember those
who it is all too willing
to easily forget.

accessory to oppression

if we allow
injustice
to happen
to one group of people
without saying anything
or fighting back

we are truly no better
than the oppressors themselves

the path of bitterness

you have the power
to determine
how you react
to the hardships
of life.

the path of bitterness
is the path
of self-hatred

which helps no one.

sorry

if he apologizes
but doesn't change
the apology
means nothing

beautiful

every
tiny detail
about you
is beautiful

<u>never</u>

never
throw away
gold
in search
of glitter

burn the fairy tales

throw all of those
ancient, misogynistic
fairy tales
into the fire

let them burn
and let
the tropes
of the damsel
in distress
and exclusively male
heroes
burn too

<u>loneliness</u>

it's easy
to need
someone
anyone

to fill
your loneliness
when midnight
strikes

but stay strong
it will pass
and you can
get through this

infinity

don't accept
bad treatment
just because
you always have

stand up
for what
you deserve

and demand
to be treated
the way
you should be

for you
are a goddess
and deserve
no less
than
infinity

<u>his</u>

you
may
be
his

but
never
forget

you
are
your
own
first
and
foremost

forget

you will never forget
the memories
you made
with him

but fear not

you will, one day
forget
the feelings you had
for him
that now sear their way
into your heart
like a branding iron

fear not
this too shall pass
and you
will
forget

<u>okay</u>

it's okay
to not
be okay

it's okay
to be

hurting
broken
hopeless
anxious
dying
devastated

just accept
the way you feel
and know this:

the sun will rise
and you
will rise
with it

<u>wolves</u>

beware
most of all
the men
who seek out
vulnerable women

to

control
abuse
hurt
manipulate

they are wolves
preying on the weak
they are evil
incarnate

do not
feed yourself
to the wolves
this
i beg of you

sometimes

sometimes
you've got to walk away
from someone
you love

because you can't love them
without hurting
yourself

<u>flower</u>

you are not
a flower
sitting pretty
smiling into
a summer breeze

you are
a fucking thunderstorm
raining vengeance
upon the wicked

<u>mirror</u>

i hate the way
i still can't smile
the way
i used to
before
i met you

<u>masterpiece</u>

you
are an unfinished work

do not compare
your prologue
to someone else's
epilogue

netflix

do not be ashamed
of needing
a day off
to sit
and relax
and put yourself
back together

mental health

if we all
treated mental health
as being
as important
as physical health

our world
would be
a lot
better off

independent

i don't want
to keep putting in hours
for someone else

i want
this book
to sell well
and i want
to live my life
in financial freedom

so please
post about this book
tell your friends
leave reviews

this
is my future
on the line

and it
is in
your hands

solidarity

i think women
need to support other women
a lot more

we turn
altogether too easily
on each other
and see each other
as enemies
when we should
be banding together
in mutual support

typewriter

there is something
so incredibly
satisfying
about the click
and clack
of a typewriter

moving across
the page
with rigid purpose
and certainty

<u>honor</u>

if nothing else
i want them
to say
she tried
her best
she did
what she could
she lived
with honor
treating others
with respect
and love

what's holding you back?

what's holding you back?
is it the past?
is it fear
of failure?

don't worry
you will
rise above
all of that
and you
will get what you want

these things
may hold you back
for now
but don't worry

everything
will be
alright

and your life
will turn out
as wonderful
as your wildest
of dreams

CHAPTER THREE

adeline whitmore

WHITE KNIGHT, DARK SOUL

white knight, dark soul

there is an epidemic
of men
who act as white knights
when the sun shines bright
and their actions are seen

but

as soon as the sun
falls below
the horizon
their true nature
is revealed

adeline whitmore

i want
the world
to fall easily
into your hands

burn the fairy tales 2

throw out
the old white men
who crowd
the seats of government
holding on
to a power
that should
have been taken
away from them
long ago

stand up
for what's right
even
when it's not
the most
popular
stance

burn the fairy tales 2

there are so many
beautiful minds
on the autism spectrum
with so much to give
to humanity

it is time
for us
to empower
their voices

adeline whitmore

humanity
is a beautiful spectrum
of sexualities
genders
minds
and personalities

burn the fairy tales 2

allow me
to touch
your soul

hold nothing
back
from me

adeline whitmore

these old men
these business tycoons
do not give a fuck
about the future

all they care about
is squeezing
a few more profits
out of the soil
of the earth
before they die

<u>love yourself</u>

love yourself
the hardest
when it is hardest
to love yourself

to be imperfect
is to be human

to be human
is to despise imperfection

but to be perfect
is not attainable

we are programmed
to hate ourselves

burn the fairy tales 2

<u>heartbeat</u>

if your heart
still beats

your story
isn't over

so keep pushing on
the sun will rise
in the morning

they may try
to keep you down
but you
are strong enough
to hold up
the collapsing sky

burn the fairy tales 2

<u>look up at the stars</u>

when the night
is silent
and full
of a heavy
darkness

that
is when its most important
to look up
at the stars

footprints

look back
at the footprints
behind you

you did that
you came this far
and you
will go
so much
further

misunderstood

she was
the brightest of flame
misunderstood
in the darkness

<u>potential</u>

never make
the mistake
of falling in love
with someone
for what you see in them
rather than
for who they are

for if you do
you will always
be disappointed

CHAPTER FOUR

HER OWN QUEEN

<u>her own queen</u>

you do not need
any ruler
except
your own
damn self

too much

you
are not
too much

one day
you will realize
you can only be
too much
to someone
who is
not enough
for you

<u>change</u>

stop complaining
about your life
and start changing
what you don't like

there is nothing

there is nothing
more beautiful
or grand

than the sight
of a woman
being
everything
she can be

<u>bloom</u>

never
be ashamed
of what you are
where you've been
or the challenges
you've faced

do not despise
the seed
from which
you bloomed

for that
is what made you
so beautiful

<u>pigs</u>

why is it
that men
always seem
to have such a hard time
saying no
to cheating

and yet
don't want women
to have the right
to say no
to them?

burn the fairy tales 2

<u>oil</u>

we flood the oceans
with oil
destroying
everything alive
within it

and yet
we remain
addicted

<u>privilege</u>

why is it so hard
for some people
to grasp
that your family's
socioeconomic status
determines
to a large extent
how far
you can go in life?

they are so blind
to their own
privilege.

military

the military
targets
the poor
and disadvantaged

they literally
want to own you

they want you to be
a modern day slave
forced to kill

just like
the colosseums

and yet
we pretend
we have advanced
as a civilization.

college/cruel jokes

colleges
are
for-profit
institutions

who will take your money
and give you
debt for life

while offering you
false promises
of freedom
and prosperity.

it is truly
a cruel joke.

burn the fairy tales 2

<u>laughter</u>

though we disagree
and make war
in different languages

laughter
knows
no language.

adeline whitmore

<u>health 'care'</u>

a medical system
that puts people
in bankruptcy
to not die
of pre-existing
conditions

is pure evil.

sophisticated puppet

it is not enough
to know
how to read.

you need to know
how to question
everything
you read
too

or else words
will make you
just a more
sophisticated
puppet.

<u>mind control</u>

i am so sick
of all the mind control
that is disguised
as

entertainment
religion
or
education

spoon-fed bullshit

we are a nation
spoon fed
propaganda
and bullshit

to fit the agenda
of a few elites.

<u>comfort</u>

we are
all too willing
to put aside
reason

for the sake
of the comfort
of false security.

pessimist

i am not
a pessimist.

i am just a realist
who is tired
of idealists
who would trade away
real change
for the sake
of vague, half-baked ideas.

complicated language

all of the
complicated language
they put
into terms of service
and contracts
is just there
to obscure the truth
and make it less obvious
that they are trying
to fuck you over.

mediocrity privilege

for too long
mediocre white men
have been allowed
to have the spotlight
on account
of their race
and gender

without a care
for the more valuable works
of real artists.

choice

abortion
is a woman's right
to control
her own body.

that is the real reason
people are against
a woman's right
to choose.

it's all about power
and oppression.

misogyny

being
lgbtq
does not excuse
misogyny.

lose-lose

i am tired
of a political system
with lose-lose options.

the lesser
of two evils
is still evil.

accept

society
is more willing
to accept
sexual abusers
than it is
to accept
transgender people.

this is a horrific hypocrisy.

endeavors

true love
is being supported
through every endeavor

and to have that
i am
eternally grateful.

simple

how people treat you
is how they
feel about you.

it's really that simple.

<u>love</u>

a mind
that supports
my dreams
and a body
that acts out
my fantasies

humble success

those who have
achieved
great success

and yet
remain humble
are very
special people.

go through hell

if we
have to go
through hell
to get
what we want

let's at least
enjoy
the journey.

<u>you</u>

even when it feels
as if the world
is on fire
and at war
with itself

you
are always there
to hold me
when things
are hard

<u>change</u>

everything
changes.

it's our job
to accept that.

<u>self</u>

it is easy
to get caught up
in struggles
of society

do not forget
to take care
of yourself

in all the small ways
that only you
know how.

adeline whitmore

BURN DOWN THE PATRIARCHY

"burn the fairy tales 2 recaptures the fiery defiance of the first book in the series while bringing a new light to self-care and self-love. burning, angry fire is met with the healing salve of coming to terms with your own traumas."

Made in the USA
Monee, IL
12 November 2019